How Many Doodles in the Pound?

R.J. Bornstein

How many doodles in the pound?

How many doodles in the pound?

I cannot count them all.

Some are big and some are small.

How many doodles in the pound?

LOST 'n'
FOUND

How many doodles in the pound?

How many doodles in the pound?

I keep going round and round,

some are lost and some are found.

How many doodles in the pound?

How many doodles in the pound?

How many doodles in the pound?

One is barking up a wall,

others make no sound at all.

How many doodles in the pound?

How many doodles in the pound?

How many doodles in the pound?

Some are slim and some are round,

some sleep completely upside down.

How many doodles in the pound?

How many doodles in the pound?

How many doodles in the pound?

Which ones chew toys? I can't recall.

One swallowed a toy, squeaker and all.

How many doodles in the pound?

How many doodles in the pound?

How many doodles in the pound?

Some ride low with belly on ground,

some grow tall, nearly cloud bound.

How many doodles in the pound?

How many doodles in the pound?

How many doodles in the pound?

These doodles are having a ball, dressed for

every season, winter, spring, summer and fall.

How many doodles in the pound?

How many doodles in the pound?

How many doodles in the pound?

Some are regal with a crown,

wagging their tails as if in London Town,

How many doodles in the pound?

How many doodles in the pound?

How many doodles in the pound?

Is there a type of counter we could install?

What say you and you and you and y'all?

How many doodles in the pound?

How many doodles in the pound?

How many doodles in the pound?

Some are laughing, some have frowns,

one is spinning round and round.

How many doodles in the pound?

There are no doodles in the pound!

There are no doodles in the pound!

I keep looking round and round.

I look up and I look down, but

There are no doodles in the pound!

Because...
they have all
been adopted!!!

Goldendoodles,

bernedoodles, sheepadoodles too.

You won't find any kind

of doodles at the zoo.

You could buy one from a breeder,

you could buy one at the mall,

but to rescue a doodle is the best choice of all.

About the author:

R.J. Bornstein and his family live in Louisville, Kentucky with their goldendoodle, Piper, the inspiration behind this endeavor.

Dedication:

Thank you to Shifrah for lending your early reading education expertise, and thank you to David and Jonathan, without whom I would never have read any books to children.

 R.J. Bornstein